**Senior Art Editor** Anna Formanek
**Project Editor** Lara Hutcheson
**Managing Editor** Tori Kosara
**Managing Art Editor** Jo Connor
**Designer** Emma Wicks
**Production Editor** Siu Yin Chan
**Senior Production Controller** Lloyd Robertson
**Publisher** Paula Regan
**Art Director** Charlotte Coulais
**Managing Director** Mark Searle

**Written by** Julia March
**Designed for DK by** Thelma-Jane Robb
**Reading Consultant** Barbara Marinak

DK would like to thank Hank Woon, Alyssa Tuffey, and the rest of the team at The Pokémon Company International. Thanks also to Lori Hand for proofreading.

First American Edition, 2025
Published in the United States by DK Publishing, a division of Penguin Random House LLC
1745 Broadway, 20th Floor, New York, NY 10019
25 26 27 28 29 10 9 8 7 6 5 4 3 2 1
001–344852–July/2025

© 2025 Pokémon. © 1995–2025 Nintendo / Creatures Inc. /
GAME FREAK inc. TM, ®, and character names are trademarks of Nintendo.

All rights reserved.
Without limiting the rights under the copyright reserved above, no part of this publication may be reproduced, stored in or introduced into a retrieval system, or transmitted, in any form, or by any means (electronic, mechanical, photocopying, recording, or otherwise), without the prior written permission of the copyright owner.
Published in Great Britain by Dorling Kindersley Limited

A catalog record for this book
is available from the Library of Congress.
ISBN 978-0-5939-6580-1 (Paperback)
ISBN 978-0-5939-6581-8 (Hardcover)

DK books are available at special discounts when purchased
in bulk for sales promotions, premiums, fund-raising, or educational use.
For details, contact: DK Publishing Special Markets,
1745 Broadway, 20th Floor, New York, NY 10019
SpecialSales@dk.com

Printed and bound in China

www.dk.com
www.pokemon.com

Level 1

# Pokémon
## Sweet Surprise

Julia March

DK

# Contents

| | |
|---|---|
| 5 | Sound it out |
| 6 | Full of surprises |
| 8 | Healing Pokémon |
| 10 | To the rescue |
| 12 | Tasty treats |
| 14 | Sweet sounds |
| 16 | Happy-go-lucky |
| 18 | Loyal friends |
| 20 | Cheerful dancers |
| 22 | Hitch a ride |
| 24 | Top teamwork |
| 26 | Gifts to share |
| 28 | Kind and caring |
| 30 | Glossary |
| 31 | Index |
| 32 | Quiz |

# Sound it out

Try saying these Pokémon names out loud.

**Alomomola**
[uh-LOH-muh-MOH-luh]

**Floette**
[Floh-ET]

**Alcremie**
[AL-kruh-mee]

**Togepi**
[TOE-ghep-pee]

**Growlithe**
[GROWL-lith]

**Pansage**
[PAN-sayj]

# Full of surprises

Pokémon are all very different.

Drampa

Drampa can stir up a sudden storm.

But they are all full of surprises!

Igglybuff

Sometimes Igglybuff can't stop bouncing.

# Healing Pokémon

Did you know that some Pokémon can heal others?

Alomomola

Golden eyes

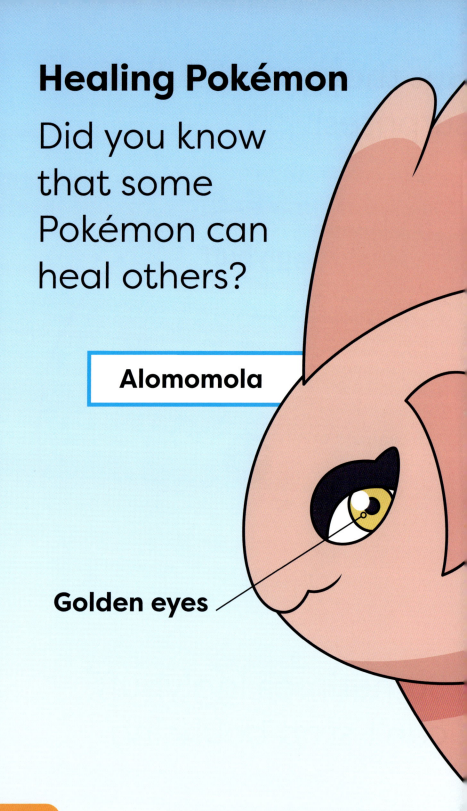

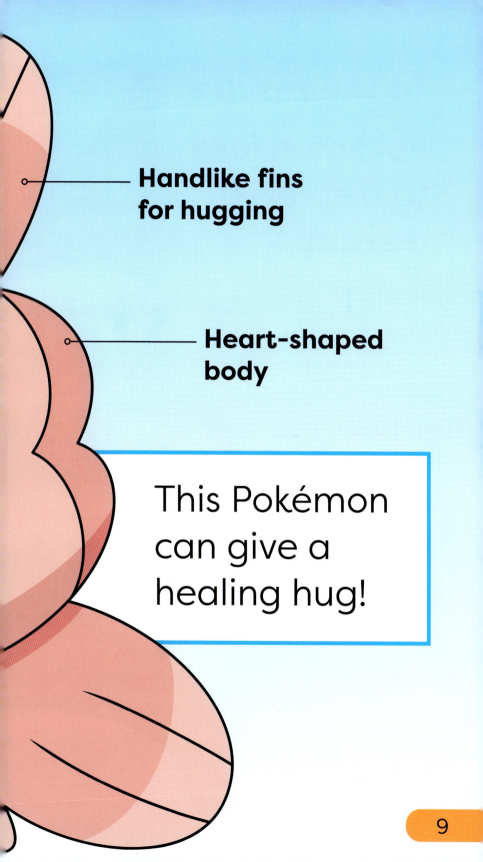

**Handlike fins for hugging**

**Heart-shaped body**

This Pokémon can give a healing hug!

# To the rescue

Pokémon love to help save the day.

**Floatzel**

**Two tails**

Floatzel rescue people who need help at sea.

Floette help limp flowers. They make them healthy.

## Tasty treats

Some Pokémon might give you a tasty surprise. A dessert made with Alcremie's sweet cream is very tasty.

**Alcremie**

**Miltank**

Miltank produce milk. Their milk changes flavor with the seasons.

# Sweet sounds

This Pokémon likes to sing among the clouds.

Short beak

Altaria

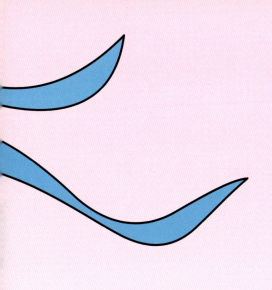

**Fluffy feathers**

They wrap friends in their wings. Then they start to sweetly hum!

# Happy-go-lucky

Find one of these Pokémon. It could bring you luck!

Togepi

Be kind to a Togepi and it will share its good luck.

Togetic can fill you with happiness.

ogetic

Togekiss

ook out
or Togekiss.
They bring blessings.

# Loyal friends

Even fierce Pokémon can be loyal friends.

**Growlithe**

Growlithe are brave Pokémon. They like to defend their friends. They will bark and bite.

**Sharp claws**

# Cheerful dancers

Watch a Pokémon dance. It will change your mood.

Brionne

Brionne's dance makes people happy.

# Sylveon

Sylveon's dance is very calming.

# Hitch a ride

Come aboard! These Pokémon are your travel buddies.

**Pelipper**

**Lapras**

Small Pokémon can hitch a ride in a Pelipper's big beak.

**Small horn**

Lapras love to carry people across the sea. If they are happy they will sing to you, too.

**Hard shell**

# Top teamwork

This pair of Pokémon like to swim together.

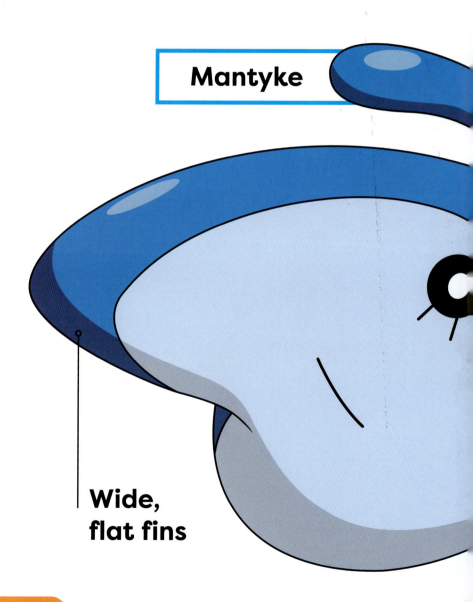

Mantyke

Wide, flat fins

**Remoraid**

Dorsal fin

They help each other avoid attacks. They also share their food.
What a great team!

25

# Gifts to share

Lots of Pokémon are happy to share their gifts.

Pachirisu

Pachirisu share electricity by rubbing their cheek pouches together.

Pansage are kind.
They share berries with
their friends.

# Kind and caring

These kind Pokémon carry a surprise!

**Happiny**

Happiny might offer their friends the white rock in their pouch.

Chansey's egg can help heal injured Pokémon.

**Chansey**

# Blissey

A bite of Blissey's egg has the power to make you smile.

# Glossary

**Blessings**
Well-wishes, or a special gift or favor.

**Limp**
Soft and weak, with no strength.

**Loyal**
Devoted and faithful to someone or something.

**Produce**
To create or to make happen.

# Index

**A**
Alcremie 12
Alomomola 8-9

**B**
Blissey 29
Brionne 20

**C**
Chansey 28

**D**
Drampa 6

**F**
Floatzel 10-11
Floette 11

**G**
Growlithe 18-19

**H**
Happiny 28

**J**
Jigglybuff 7

**L**
Lapras 23

**M**
Mantyke 24-25
Miltank 13

**P**
Pachirisu 26
Pansage 27
Pelipper 22

**R**
Remoraid 25

**S**
Sylveon 21

**T**
Togekiss 17
Togepi 16
Togetic 17

31

# Quiz

Ready to find out how much you learned? Read the questions and then check your answers with an adult.

1. Can Drampa stir up a storm?
2. Which Pokémon produces milk?
3. How do Alomomola heal Pokémon?
4. Do Growlithe sometimes bark and bite?
5. What do Lapras do if they are happy?

1. Yes  2. Miltank  3. With a gentle hug  4. Yes  5. Sing